SPOONS AND FORKS, ELECTRO SILVER PLATED ON BEST NICKEL SILVER

No. 6385 Engraved Old English Pattern. Dessert Fork

No. 6384

No. 6383 Fiddle Pattern. Dessert Fork

D0532134

WITHDRAWN

No. 6388 Beaded Pattern. Table Spoon

No. 6387 Thread and Shell Pattern. Dessert Fork

No. 6386 Rat Tail Pattern. Dessert Spoon

FORKS, KNIVES & SPOONS

FORKS KNIVES & SPOONS

Peri Wolfman and Charles Gold

Photographs by Charles Gold

CLARKSON POTTER/PUBLISHERS

NEW YORK

FRONTISPIECE: *Bone-handled steel fork and knife.*
OPPOSITE: *A jumble of silver-plate spoons.*
PAGE 6: *An elaborate two-sided olive fork-spoon of silver over brass, circa 1880, was made by Gorham.*

Design by

JENNIFER NAPIER

Published by Clarkson Potter/Publishers, 201 East 50th Street, New York, New York 10022. Member of the Crown Publishing Group.

Random House, Inc. New York, Toronto, London, Sydney, Auckland

CLARKSON N. POTTER, POTTER, and colophon are trademarks of Clarkson N. Potter, Inc.

Manufactured in China

Library of Congress Cataloging-in-Publication Data
Wolfman, Peri. Forks, knives, and spoons/Peri Wolfman and Charles Gold:
Photographs by Charles Gold.
Includes index.
1. Cookery. 2. Flatware--History. 3. Flatware--Collectors and collecting. I.
Gold, Charles. II Title.
TX714.W643 1994
642'.6--dc20 93-39991 CIP
ISBN 0-517-58828-5
10 9 8 7 6 5 4 3

To my sisters, Laurie, Bonnie, and Cathy,
without whom I would have all the family forks,
knives, and spoons. And to Charley Gold, my
partner in all things in this life,
including some pretty terrific battles of wills.
He remains collaborator, photographer, stylist,
chef, father, and best boyfriend
par excellence. — P.W.

To Peri, who showed me another way.
With love — C.G.

CONTENTS

ACKNOWLEDGMENTS

As anyone who has ever compiled a book of photographs and words will tell you, it's a team effort. Each and every person we are thanking here has left a thumbprint on the forks, knives, and spoons in this volume.

To all of our friends who have shared their beautiful cutlery with us, and often a meal to match, thank you!

In the United States: Bunny Williams and John Rosselli of Treillage; Tricia Foley of the Bellport General Store; Mindy Papp of Florian Papp Antiques; Susan Rosenfeld and Peter Hoffman of Savoy; Barbara Stratton of Jerry's; Bruce and Eric Bromberg of the Blue Ribbon; Ina Garten of the Barefoot Contessa in East Hampton; Michael Ballon of Castle Street Cafe in the Berkshires; Mark and Christi Carter of the Carter House in Eureka, California; Howard and Gail Adler of The Good Cooks Club; and Marnie Carmichael, who makes the best damn pound cake on earth.

In London: Kate Dyson of the Dining Room Shop; and Camilla, Annabel, and Michael of Emporio Armani.

In Paris: Marie Ange Bon of DOT; Christine de Beaupré of Paris je t'aime; and Aude Clément of Au Bain Marie for their fabulous French flair.

To the experts who graciously shared their special interest and knowledge of forks, knives, and spoons: Edward Munvees and family of James Robinson silversmiths; Sheila Chefetz of Country Dining Room Antiques; Gerri Bowman of Christofle; Donna Ferrari of *Bride's* magazine; Mrs. Hagerty of the 100-year-old W. J. Hagerty and Sons, Ltd; Edith Gillson of Cupboards and Roses Antiques; Jean Cherneff of Ashley Falls Antiques; and Moya Smith and all of her English silverware!

To our great little team of fresh-out-of-college smarty-pants: Sarah Durham, who set up my Mac and taught me to use it (wow, I love it!); Lily Genis, who haunted the New York Public Library in search of snippets of obscure information; and Alexander Wolfman, whose research and editing proved that all the money that went into his education was worth every penny!

To our home team at Wolfman•Gold, headed by Sharron Lewis and Beaty Eng, whose competence and loyalty gave us the time to work on this book. To Karen Russo, for bringing us just the right book; and to Lois Granger at the studio for arranging all of those sustaining lunches.

To our agents, past and present, Pam Bernstein and Michael Carlisle, for making a good marriage with Clarkson Potter.

Then there's the whole team at Clarkson Potter who edited, designed, and made a book happen from our jumble of pictures and words. Thanks to Jennifer Napier and her wonderful taste; to Chesie Hortenstine and her winning ways.

A very special thank-you to Roy Finamore and Howard Klein, whose personal interest in this book has pushed us, unmercifully, to a new level in photography and styling.

OVERLEAF: *An antique cast-iron urn is filled with an array of vintage cutlery. The ornate Victorian serving fork and spoon are American sterling.*

PREFACE

I LOVE FORKS, knives, and spoons. They're like grown-up toys for the table. Over the years I've made a collection of silver-plate cutlery. It started with a gift from my stepmother, Elsie, of silver-plated fish forks, fish knives, and European dessert spoons that had been handed down to her by her grandmother. These jewels of the table came with a rich history—of Elsie's grandmother, proprietor of the Hotel New York in Marienbad, Czechoslovakia, and her stories of European royalty dining with these very same pieces of cutlery in the elegant years of the early 1900s.

This little piece of history whetted my appetite, and I just couldn't stop collecting. I began searching the farthest corners of flea markets, antique shops, and antique shows. On summer weekends in New England, I make Charley get up at the crack of dawn to be among the first at the gate of each and every antique show within driving distance. I look forward with anticipation to what I may find on the tables set up in fields or in the red barns. It may be a set of bone-handled knives with rusted steel blades, or wood-handled forks with decorative steel rivets, a collection of delicate coin silver teaspoons, or a set of 1930s stainless steel spoons with bright Bakelite handles. We race from dealer to dealer, with a paper cup of our first morning coffee and maybe a forbidden doughnut. It's so American.

Then in the dead of winter, after the Christmas rush is over and there's a lull in my New York City shop, I have an overriding need to shop the antique markets in London. The nastier the weather, the more heightened is my sense of adventure. In London, we have the best chance of coming across armfuls of real treasures. Here I search for sets of tea knives with colorful resin handles and silver cuffs, old hotel silver plate with fat hollow handles, and fish servers with elaborate chasing on the silver. Charley searches out the more bizarre Victorian utensils like marrow spoons, ham bone holders, and bread forks. When dawn starts to break and we're chilled to the bone, we nip into the antique dealers' favorite cafe for a real English breakfast of fried eggs, "bubble and squeak," and fried tomatoes served on heavy dinner plates and eaten with truly terrible, bent-out-of-shape stainless steel forks. While we warm up in this steamy congenial place, we talk with fellow dealers and buyers of the fabulous Victorian cutlery we just bought. It's so English.

In Paris, we shop at the tableware shows for new European silver plate, colorful plastic-handled stainless steel sets, and salad servers made of resin that imitate the antique, typically French bone and horn

PAGE 12: *While making the join of the bowl and handle on the back of a 19th-century pewter serving spoon, the craftsman added a decorative element.* ABOVE: *Early 20th-century hollow-handle fruit forks and scallop bowl dessert spoons.*

servers. Then for fun we search the Marché aux Puces and the shops around the Place des Vosges for real silver, stopping at a sidewalk cafe for a *café au lait* and croissants. It's so French.

Just as there has been a new interest in food in America over the last decade, so has there been a renewed interest in tableware. Restaurants, not just the three- and four-star variety, are using fish forks and knives— usually bringing them to the table with the proper course to eliminate "cutlery confusion." They are also bringing sauce spoons with a first course, main course, or dessert that's sauced. But of all the things we use on the table, cutlery (or silverware) strikes the most fear in the heart of the American diner. Most of us were not brought up with a strict set of rules guiding table manners as were our European peers, and the sight of three forks, three knives, and two spoons can be a social fright. Fortunately, it's a fright easily overcome by remembering that cutlery is used from the outside in. Of course, that assumes that your host also knows that rule, and has set the table accordingly.

It serves us well to know the rules of etiquette. But this American of the 20th cent-

At the crack of dawn at Bermondsey Market, Moya Smith is ready to chat and to sell her English silver wares.

ury is allowed to break the rules, just a little! I sometimes use fish forks and knives for dessert, a bread fork for pot roast, or a bonbon spoon for tomatoes. I've never had anyone at our dinner table cry out in horror over this misuse of tools—probably because not many of our friends know what their original intended use was.

The proper Victorians had a specialized utensil for every conceivable food so they would never have to touch anything with their hands. One night at a friend's small dinner party, conversation turned to eccentric Victorian cutlery, and escalated into "Can you top this?" I knew I had them when I asked if anyone knew what the original use was of the fork our hostess had placed on the tomato platter. It was something like a spoon, but with four short tines cut from the top. There was a lot of guessing. A berry spoon? An ice-cream fork? A cucumber server? No, no, I informed them, it's a terrapin fork, used for eating turtle broth and meat! I thought I had won. Then one of the guests said she had a "runcible" spoon.

I couldn't wait to get home to my reference books. It wasn't in any of them. The library was next, and finally the dictionary. There it was, *runcible spoon,* a nonsense word coined in the 1870s by Edward Lear in "The Owl and the Pussy-Cat," which has been applied to a sharp-edged, broad-pronged pickle fork:

> They dined on mince, with slices of quince,
> Which they ate with a runcible spoon,
> And hand in hand, on the edge of the sand,
> They danced by the light of the moon.

In our fascination with the obscure single-use forks, knives, and spoons of the Victorian years, Charley and I have talked to dealers in all the antique stores and shows that we have scoured. We have exchanged information about the most peculiar implements whose intended use can be a matter of considerable speculation. In the process, we have gathered a modicum of knowledge and a lot of cutlery. Because of its variety and proliferation, Victorian cutlery, especially silver plate, is fun to shop for, affordable to collect, and a welcome addition to any dinner table.

It is our pleasure to share with you not only what we have learned of the history and evolution of antique cutlery, but also the way our collected cutlery fits the foods we eat today. Our favorite tables are set with unmatched cutlery—a silver dinner fork and knife, a Victorian bone-handled fish fork and knife, and an oversized English dessert spoon—and a meal to match it all.

And since we do believe that a picture is worth a thousand words, my photographer husband, Charley Gold, and I want to share with you, in pictures and words, some of our favorite foods and recipes served up with some of our favorite forks, knives, and spoons.

—PERI WOLFMAN

Sugar and ice tongs hang from a clothesline, and faux ivory–handled knives are bundled on a table. All await buyers at Bermondsey Market.

Fig. 653 à 656. — Modèles

A LITTLE HISTORY

THE SPOON IS thought to be the oldest of the three basic eating implements. The first spoon was probably a shell lashed to a stick, which made scooping water from river or stream more efficient than using a cupped hand. With man's discovery of fire and cooked foods, spoons carved of wood evolved. These first spoons were used not for eating, but for stirring hot foods. Soup was drunk from a bowl long before people thought to use a spoon for *eating* soup.

During the Middle Ages, spoons and knives were considered

objects of great value. Starting in the 13th century, they were even included in the wills and household inventories of the rich. From these lists we know that spoons were carved from such woods as boxwood, juniper, poplar, and cherry. Others were cast of bronze, gold, or silver.

The earliest spoons had fig-shaped bowls which were round in the front and pointed toward the handle. The oval-shaped soup spoon, so common today, didn't develop until the 17th century. This was the only spoon shape that existed until the latter part of that century, when coffee and tea arrived in Europe. Then smaller spoons of silver or gold, for stirring sugar into coffee and tea, started to show up in the royal courts of France.

Not until the Victorian era in the late 19th century was there any further development of the spoon. When the English fell in love with the idea of an abundance of unusual foods at their banquet and dinner tables, they found it necessary to create a

PAGE 18: *Antique Victorian silver serving forks, knives, and trowels all have hollow handles.* RIGHT: *Spoons for all reasons: slender marrow spoons, coin silver tea and serving spoons, a bone honey spoon with silver handle, a carved ivory serving spoon, and a collection of silver tablespoons.*

piece of silver cutlery to convey each food from service plate to dinner plate and then from dinner plate to mouth. It was at this time in history that the simple oval table-spoon ceased to be the all-purpose eating tool that it had been for centuries, and spoons proliferated in all shapes and sizes. There were spoons invented for every kind of soup, spoons for sauces, for citrus fruits, for berries, and for puddings. There were spoons for coffee and tea and four o'clock tea and iced tea, and spoons for tomatoes, for aspic, and for olives. Spoons for retriev-

The American pewter porridge spoon was made in the style of the 17th-century Pilgrim pattern.

ing marrow from a bone, and spoons for scooping servings of Stilton cheese. Given this opulence, we might come to the erroneous conclusion that every man was born with a silver spoon in his mouth.

The knife had its beginning as a tool and a weapon rather than as an eating utensil. Since solid food could be eaten with the fingers, it wasn't until people started to eat hot food that we required a utensil to keep from being burned.

In the Middle Ages, people brought their own eating tools—which might have included a spoon, but always a knife—to the table. Early knives were daggerlike with two sharp edges for cutting and a sharp point at the end for spearing food and bringing it to the mouth.

In the 17th century, to prevent men from stabbing one another while dining, Cardinal Richelieu of France decreed it illegal for cutlers to make pointed dinner knives for innkeepers. This signaled the evolution of the knife from a sharp-pointed weapon, to the rounded-end table knife with only one cutting edge that we know today.

In the 11th century, according to a romantic Italian story, a wealthy Venetian doge, while traveling in the Middle East,

Late 19th-century steel knives and forks have bone handles riveted to their steel shanks with decorative designs.

met and married a beautiful Turkish princess. The princess brought back with her to Venice a case of golden table forks with which she had eaten all her life. The princess's forks created an outrage that shocked the church leaders of Venice. "God in his wisdom has provided man with natural forks," they said, "his fingers." Others called her forks "luxurious beyond belief." But by the 14th century it was common for European royalty to have one table fork, with a set of knives to be used communally. Two centuries later Catherine de' Médici, the Italian wife of King Henry II, introduced the use of one table fork for each diner to the French court. But even then it was still thought to be an affectation.

Rounded steel knife blades were used for transporting food from plate to mouth as late as the 19th century.

In 1611 the English writer Thomas Coryate claimed to be the first man in London to eat with a fork, which he had brought back from his travels in Italy. In a book entitled *Crudities Hastily Gobbled Up in Five Months,* he wrote:

> *This form of eating I understand is generally used in all places of Italy; their forks being for the most part made of iron or steel, and some of silver, but those are used only by gentlemen.*

Other travelers to Italy wrote of "pasta being fork lifted to the mouth."

As late as the 18th century, most Englishmen were still using their knife like a flat spoon, to bring food to their mouth. There is an anonymous English poem that must have been inspired by this lingering habit:

> *I eat my peas with honey,*
> *I've done it all my life;*
> *It makes the peas taste funny,*
> *But it keeps them on my knife.*

The Americans held on to the habit of eating with a knife until the end of the 19th century. An American newspaper published the anonymous complaint: "Eating peas with a fork is as bad as trying to eat soup with a knitting needle." It remains a mystery why eating peas with a spoon was never considered proper.

With new manufacturing techniques and the demand among the new rich for more elaborate and specialized pieces of cutlery, manufacturers produced sets of matched silverware that included as many as 140 distinct and different pieces. These sets came in fitted chests often as big as a man. In collecting Victorian cutlery today, it is rare to find whole large sets still intact. Yet specialized sets that are not a part of a matched pattern, such as fish eaters and dessert sets, dessert spoons and coffee spoons, are abundant. It is interesting to find that the centuries-old habit of pairing the fork and knife still remains but that the spoon stands alone.

With the end of the extravagances of the industrial age, and the onset of the practicalities of modern life, table cutlery became downright boring. In 1926 the American Sterling Silverware Manufacturers adopted a list of 55 items as the greatest number of separate pieces that would be made in any single pattern, and it has dwindled from there. Today—with the exception of a few silversmiths, such as James Robinson, who produce up to twenty-five pieces in a single pattern—we are down to the basic five-piece place setting, which includes only a dinner fork and knife and a smaller fork to be used for salad, dessert, lunch, and breakfast. That leaves two spoons: a soup spoon and a tea spoon, to do the work of a dozen ancestors. How practical. And how boring! What a good reason to make use of our grandmothers' heirloom silver, or to collect and create heirlooms of our own choosing from the generous legacy left us by the Victorians.

Sterling silver serving spoons in the Art Nouveau style.

COIN SILVER

In England and in America, there were spoons made of *coin silver* from the 17th century until the industrial age in the 19th century. The earliest coin silver was in fact made by melting down coins into ingots and then hammering the ingots into sheets to be formed into spoons and sometimes forks. In England, the coins were of sterling silver with 925 parts of silver to 1,000. In America, coin silver had the same degree of purity as the American silver dollar, which was 900 parts of silver to 1,000. Later coin silver was made with the same proportion of pure silver to alloy, but no longer of melted coins.

Whole first names, as well as last names and elaborate monograms, were often engraved on coin silver spoons.

THE SILVER STANDARD

*We will make thee borders of gold
with studs of silver.*
—THE SONG OF SOLOMON

The silver standard was instituted by King Edward I of England in the 14th century. In order to be described as silver, spoons and other objects had to contain at least 925 parts of silver out of 1,000 parts, the balance being an alloy, usually copper. The king ordered the wardens of Goldsmiths' Hall to examine all silver objects to be sure they met the standard. Those that passed the test were stamped with a "hallmark" on the back of the stem. There was a distinct mark for each city, each silversmith, and each year. In researching a piece of early English silver, it is best to consult an authoritative book (see page 139) on silver hallmarks, since there are so many marks and variations.

Sterling silver serving forks from the same silversmith were offered in two different "patterns."

CAST OF CUTLERY

*"How did you think I managed a
dinner, Clarence?"
"Capitally!"
"I had a knife and two forks left at the
end," she said regretfully.*
—WILLIAM PETT RIDGE

Emily Post's rule is that "no more than three of any one utensil be set down at a place setting at one time. If more are necessary, they are to be brought to the table with the course for which they are intended."

For those of us who like to entertain at dinner, the abbreviated five-piece setting is a little too skimpy. We always need extra small forks for salad and dessert; we need extra small spoons if dessert is to be coffee and ice cream. Of course we're not suggesting that it is necessary to have the ten forks, eleven spoons, or eight knives pictured on the following pages when only a few of each would produce a well-set table. But it can be amusing to select from a lavish array of cutlery left from an age of innocence.

SEAFOOD OR
HORS D'OEUVRES
FORK

OYSTER
FORK

SNAIL
FORK

LOBSTER
FORK

PASTRY
FORK

DESSERT
FORK

SALAD
FORK

FISH
FORK

LUNCHEON
FORK

DINNER
FORK

DINNER
KNIFE

LUNCHEON
KNIFE

SALAD
KNIFE

CHEESE
KNIFE

BUTTER
KNIFE

FISH
KNIFE

STEAK
KNIFE

FRUIT
KNIFE

DESSERT
SPOON

TABLESPOON

ICED TEA
SPOON

SAUCE
SPOON

CREAM SOUP
SPOON

BOUILLON
SPOON

CITRUS
SPOON

COFFEE
SPOON

TEA
SPOON

ICE CREAM
SPOON

DEMITASSE
SPOON

STARTERS

THIS IS WHERE the real fun starts—collecting and dining with some of the hundreds of different forks and knives that were laid on the tables in the homes of the new rich in the late 19th century. Since a proper dinner began with fish, there were not just little three-pronged seafood forks, but oyster forks with short fat tines and snail forks with long, curved skinny tines. There were lobster forks with tines that imitated a lobster's claws, and terrapin forks that were half spoon, half fork, and sardine forks with short wide tines for lifting the little fish but not breaking them.

Of course, sets of fish forks and knives and fish servers were part of every proper table setting. If the handles weren't silver, they might be

carved ivory, bone, or mother-of-pearl.
Their blades and tines were of silver or silver plate. And to show that the only purpose of the knife was to gently debone cooked fish, the blades were not sharp. They were, however, extravagantly or whimsically designed, often in the shape of a fish.

In the 1920s, copies of these original fish sets were produced with blades and tines of stainless steel and handles of faux bone or ivory, making them available to the growing middle class.

All of these "fish eaters" are treasures worth hunting for in antique shops and markets, and they are certain to add a little of the history of a more elegant time to the tables we set today.

PAGE 36: *Fish servers with elaborately carved handles; their silver tines and blades are chased and pierced. At the base of the cast-iron urn is a serving trowel, circa 1906.* RIGHT: *The elaborately ornate set of sterling silver fish servers has hollow handles. The tines and blade are pierced and decorated with chasing. Made in Sheffield, England, circa 1871.*

PASTA WITH CAVIAR

*If you love caviar as much as we do,
you'll enjoy this new twist on an
extravagant treat. Use a bone or horn spoon
for serving caviar from the tin.
A silver fish fork with a bone, horn,
or mother-of-pearl handle would look extra special
with this pasta.*

*½ pound fresh angel-hair pasta
½ cup unsalted butter
4 ounces Sevruga caviar, or any
good caviar*

Cook the pasta until al dente in salted boiling water. Drain, toss with butter, and arrange on individual plates. Top each with a good dollop of caviar.

SERVES 4

CAVIAR SPOONS

It is more than a food; it is a dream.
—CHRISTIAN PETROSSIAN

Caviar, more than any other food, evokes images of luxury and celebration, of tables set with burnished silver and glasses sparkling amid candlelight. In the 17th century, Louis XIV served caviar at his Paris table, and the czars of Russia indulged in caviar fished from the Caspian Sea.

Connoisseurs prefer to eat caviar off of a spoon to get its full taste. But exactly what spoon is most important, since the taste of caviar is spoiled by contact with metal, even precious silver or gold. For centuries, spoons of carved horn, bone, and mother-of-pearl have been made especially for use in the ritual of caviar.

LEFT: *The elegant Trifid pattern sterling is made today by James Robinson in England.* OPPOSITE: *A small sampling of caviar spoons.*

CASTLE STREET CAFE
ZUCCHINI FRITTERS

In Great Barrington, Massachusetts, Michael Ballon makes good use of summer's bounty with this easy starter. We think antique "fish eaters" are the ideal size and shape for fritters.

3 medium zucchini, grated
1 tablespoon coarse salt
1 small onion, peeled and grated
2 eggs, lightly beaten
⅓ cup flour
½ teaspoon of chopped thyme
Olive oil
Crème fraîche

Toss the zucchini with the coarse salt. Place in a colander with a weight on top and let stand in the sink for 30 minutes in order to drain off the liquid.

Transfer the zucchini to a mixing bowl. Add the onion, eggs, flour, and thyme and mix well.

Warm 1 tablespoon of olive oil in a non-stick skillet over medium heat. When hot, ladle in enough batter for 1 large or 2 small fritters. Cook until golden, about 1 minute on each side. Heat more oil and repeat.

Serve with a dollop of crème fraîche.

SERVES 4

OPPOSITE: *Zucchini fritters. Made in Sheffield, England, of silver plate over brass, the hollow-handle set has acquired a warm glow.* ABOVE: *The new French silver cheese knife has a blade sharp enough for cutting and two prongs for picking up a chunk of aged cheese.*

SAUCES FOR SMOKED FISH

Simple, low-calorie sauces for any smoked fish. Both sauces can be kept, refrigerated, for about a week.

HORSERADISH SAUCE

1 cup plain low-fat yogurt

1 jar (6 ounces) white horseradish, drained

1 teaspoon sugar

MUSTARD SAUCE

½ cup Dijon mustard

½ cup rough mustard

1 tablespoon Coleman's dry mustard

3 tablespoons dark brown sugar

½ cup fresh dill, finely chopped

Mix all ingredients. Then refrigerate for 1 hour or more.

EACH MAKES ABOUT 1 CUP

FAVA BEANS

The fat, light beans remind us of Tuscany. They're a great way to welcome spring, especially when served with a vintage slotted berry spoon.

2 pounds fava beans, shelled

Extra-virgin olive oil

Salt and pepper

4 garlic cloves, chopped

12 sage leaves, chopped, and 1 sprig

6 scallions, sliced in rounds

Place the favas in a pot and cover with well-salted water. Bring to boil. Boil 5 minutes, drain, and place in a serving bowl. Drizzle with olive oil and add salt and pepper to taste. Toss with the garlic, chopped sage, and scallions. Garnish with a sprig of sage.

SERVES 6 AS A SIDE DISH

OPPOSITE TOP: *This silver-plate, hollow-handle fish set came from my great-grandmother's hotel in Marienbad in the early 1900s. Here, it is used with a salad of smoked fish and two sauces.*
OPPOSITE BOTTOM: *It is likely that the Bakelite handle on this decorative silver-bowl berry spoon was a replacement for the original ivory or bone handle.*

BREAD KNIVES

Give us this day our daily bread.
— THE GOSPEL ACCORDING TO
ST. MATTHEW

At French tables, bread is broken, not cut—
partly because it is supposed to be too tender to need cutting. If bread is served
sliced, it is cut in the kitchen, away from the
dinner table. An antique French bread knife
would be a very utilitarian tool, indeed.

But bread that is sliced for buttering or
toasting requires knives for slicing as well as
knives for spreading butter or jam.

It is likely that a knife with the word
"BREAD" carved into its wooden handle is of
English or Irish origin. Antique bread
knives with natural horn or decoratively
carved ivory or bone handles were probably
produced in England, Ireland, or Germany.
Rare indeed is a bread knife with a silver
handle; surely it was used at the dinner
table of a fine English manor house.

English bread knives with handles of hollow silver, carved
wood, and cross-hatched bone—all with Sheffield steel blades.

SARDINE FORKS

The Victorian obsession for having a special utensil for each and every food is no more evident than in the large variety of sardine forks that can still be found at the antiques markets in London.

With five broad and gently curved tines, these forks could lift the little fish from serving platter to individual plate without breaking them.

The tines were always silver or silver plate, ensuring that the fresh lemon squeezed over the fish would not impart a metallic taste. It isn't difficult to identify a sardine fork. Many have the word "sardine" carved into the handle; others have little fish engraved at the base of the tines. But even without these obvious clues, the tines will announce the fork's use.

We put these amusing forks to use serving sliced meats and fish like prosciutto, salami, and smoked salmon.

ABOVE: *Both sardine forks have little fish engraved on the tines; one handle is horn; the other is of carved wood.*

SHARRON'S TOMATO ONION CHUTNEY

Almost cooks itself, lasts forever, and keeps on giving! It's a fine accompaniment to ham. It also makes a great gift—presented in a glass jar with an antique silver spoon tied on with a ribbon.

12 *large tomatoes, ripe but firm*
4 *large onions*
2 *tablespoons salt*
2 *cups brown sugar*
3 *chili peppers, coarsely chopped*
Red wine vinegar
2 *tablespoons flour*
1 *tablespoon curry powder*
1 *tablespoon Coleman's dry mustard*

We like to serve Sharron Lewis's chutney from a footed glass using a small silver ladle or a coin silver tea spoon.

Peel the tomatoes and cut them in large chunks. Peel the onions and cut them in large chunks. Combine both vegetables in a ceramic or glass bowl, sprinkle with the salt, cover, and leave overnight.

The next day, pour off the liquid. Put the tomatoes and onions in a large, heavy saucepan with the brown sugar and chilies. Add enough vinegar to cover. Bring to a boil and simmer for 1½ hours.

Mix the flour, curry powder, and mustard with a little vinegar to make a smooth paste. Stir it into the tomato mixture and bring to a boil. Boil for 5 minutes, let cool, and serve at room temperature.

To store, ladle into 4 sterilized quart jars and seal tightly. Keep refrigerated.

MAKES 3 TO 4 QUARTS

THE BLUE RIBBON'S
SEAFOOD CONDIMENTS

MIGNONETTE SAUCE
5 shallots, diced
3 cups red wine vinegar
3 cups sherry vinegar
¼ cup balsamic vinegar
2 tablespoons cracked black pepper

Combine all the ingredients and let sit in the refrigerator for at least 1 hour before serving.

TOPPING
3 tablespoons dry parsley
1 tablespoon dry garlic
2 tablespoons dry onion
4 tablespoons salt
3 tablespoons dry basil
2 tablespoons dry thyme
2 teaspoons cayenne
1 teaspoon white pepper

SPICY MAYONNAISE
4 egg yolks
1 whole egg
2 shallots, diced
3 tablespoons Dijon mustard
2 cups olive oil
1 cup peanut oil

⅛ cup red wine vinegar
Salt and pepper

To make the Topping: Combine all of the ingredients, and set aside.

To make the Spicy Mayonnaise: Combine the egg yolks, whole egg, shallots, and mustard. Slowly whisk in the oils to achieve a thick, creamy sauce. Thin with the vinegar and season with salt and pepper. When ready to serve, sprinkle the topping over the mayonnaise.

ALONSO SAUCE
1 branch celery, diced
½ onion, diced
1 tomato, seeded and diced
1 bunch cilantro, chopped
3 cups lemon juice
2 shots hot sauce
1 teaspoon salt
1 teaspoon cracked black pepper

Combine all of the ingredients and let sit in the refrigerator for ½ hour before serving.

The French silver lobster fork has long skinny tines for winkling out the meat from the shell. The Blue Ribbon condiments are in individual bowls.

TOP: *The curved tines of an oyster fork help loosen the oyster from its shell.* ABOVE: *An array of silver-plate forks for eating escargot, lobster, oysters, and seafood cocktail. The first three are new French Christofle; the last is American from the 1920s.*

EMPORIO ARMANI CARPACCIO

Here's a great place to put to use your Victorian dessert forks and knives. This salad is easy to assemble and pretty to look at, and it makes a satisfying starter for dinner, or a whole lunch.

1 large bunch arugula
1 pound beef fillet, sliced paper thin
4 shiitake mushrooms, thinly sliced
4 oyster mushrooms, thinly sliced
2 lemons, cut in half
Salt and pepper
Extra-virgin olive oil
Parmesan cheese

Cut the arugula in very fine strips and pile it in the center of individual salad plates. Layer 3 slices of beef over the greens and top with one slice of each mushroom.

Squeeze ½ lemon over each salad, and season with salt and pepper. Drizzle with the olive oil, top with a few shavings of Parmesan, and serve.

SERVES 4

Armani-designed dinner forks and knives—here with the carpaccio—mirror 18th-century bone and steel cutlery.

Length, 6 inches.

SOUPS

WHEN WE SIT down to dinner and soup is served, there is no
question as to which piece of cutlery to use.

The oval-shaped tablespoon, so familiar to us today, developed in
the 17th century and remains the spoon of many uses. By the 18th
century it became conventional in Europe to "eat" soup with a spoon
instead of drinking it from a shallow bowl. By the 19th century, in
Victorian England, there was a different-shaped spoon for every
soup. There was a small round-bowl spoon for bouillon, a larger
round-bowl spoon for creamed soup, and a large oval-bowl spoon for
soups with chunks of vegetables or meat.

Almost a century later, we have inherited a large array of spoons that can be used for soup—and a lot of confusion over for what each was originally intended.

The European dessert spoon was made so that Englishmen might eat their puddings. You can find these spoons in the antique markets of London, with elaborately decorated handles and extra-large oval bowls. They are big and beautiful and perfect for eating a hearty soup. This spoon is especially suited to collecting in different patterns, mixing, matching, and using them together.

The American tablespoon is good for eating soup or serving vegetables. And, of course, the American soup spoon, a smaller version of the tablespoon, is very multipurpose, and all soups can be eaten with it.

But why spoil the fun by limiting your table to one spoon for all soups? You can use a beautiful round-bowl spoon for eating creamy soups, like corn chowder or butternut squash soup. It is especially elegant in a simple sterling silver pattern like Queen Anne.

The smaller round-bowl bouillon spoons are not often found on their own, but usually turn up as part of a large set of silverware. A bouillon spoon could be confused with a baby spoon or jam spoon, if it weren't for the longer length of the handle. Traditionally used for the clear soups, like consommé, it is great to use for any soup served in a small bowl or mug.

Soup spoons are not without their traditions. An old English Christmas custom was for all diners to hold up their soup spoons before starting their meal and, as with a toast, to wish health to absent friends.

PAGE 54: *A variety of silver soup spoons—old and new, ornate and simple—in an antique glazed terra-cotta urn.* OPPOSITE: *Circa 1860 English silver dessert spoons are ornately decorated, front and back, top and bottom.*

JERRY'S VERY VEGETABLE BEAN SOUP

A hearty soup requires a hearty tablespoon or cream soup spoon.

¼ cup olive oil
2 medium yellow onions, chopped
8 garlic cloves, peeled and minced
2 stalks celery, diced
2 carrots, peeled and diced
1 teaspoon dried basil
1 teaspoon dried thyme
1 teaspoon red pepper flakes
1 large can plum tomatoes with juice
4 cups water
2 cups new potatoes, medium diced
2 cups white beans
2 cups lima beans or any similar bean
Salt and pepper

1 small bunch parsley, chopped
1 cup torn fresh spinach leaves
Fresh Parmesan cheese

Heat the oil in a large saucepan over medium heat. Add the onions and garlic and sauté briefly. Add the celery, carrots, basil, thyme, and red pepper flakes. Sauté for 10 minutes. Add the plum tomatoes, water, and potatoes and bring to a simmer. Add the white beans and lima beans. Simmer gently until the potatoes are cooked, 20 to 30 minutes. Season with salt, pepper, and parsley.

Serve in individual bowls, topped with torn spinach leaves and shavings of Parmesan.

SERVES 8 TO 10

ABOVE: *James Robinson silversmiths made this sterling silver cream soup spoon in the English Trifid pattern.*

SUMMER VEGETABLE SOUP

We like to eat this soup with large European dessert spoons or tablespoons— taking full advantage of summer's fresh vegetable bounty.

4 cups chicken broth

3 cups water

2 cups white wine

2 garlic cloves, finely chopped

1 small head green cabbage, chopped coarsely

1 large zucchini, quartered lengthwise, then cut across into ½-inch slices

4 ears fresh corn, kernels cut and cobs scraped

½ pound fresh sorrel, coarsely chopped

Salt and pepper

Place the chicken broth, water, wine, and garlic in a stockpot and bring to a boil. Add the cabbage and zucchini, bring back to the boil, reduce the heat, and simmer for 5 minutes. Add the corn and most of the sorrel and simmer for 2 minutes longer. Season with salt and pepper to taste. Serve hot.

This is also wonderful chilled. Let it cool in the pot, refrigerate it, and remove any fat that congeals on the surface. Serve sprinkled with chopped sorrel.

SERVES 8

ABOVE: *A fancy Victorian silver dessert spoon pairs well with vegetable soup in a simple porcelain bowl.*

BERTHA'S BUTTERNUT SQUASH SOUP

This rich-tasting soup with no fat and few calories makes a great winter lunch. To spoon up the golden, velvety soup, use a silver tablespoon.

2 medium butternut squash, peeled, seeded, and cut into chunks
3 apples, peeled, cored, and cut into chunks
2 onions, peeled and diced
2 cups chicken broth
3 tablespoons curry powder
Salt and pepper

Combine all the ingredients in a stockpot and add water to cover. Bring to a simmer and cook for 40 minutes.

Blend in a food processor, then return to the pot and reheat.

Serve with a dollop of yogurt.

SERVES 6 TO 8

ABOVE: *A pair of English silver-plate soup ladles in the King's pattern and a sterling ladle in the classic Fiddle pattern.*
OPPOSITE: *Large oval-bowl silver dessert spoons. Some match; some don't. All are fine when eating squash soup.*

Contemporary stainless steel cutlery with marblized plastic handles, set in the French style, facing down.

FRENCH SETTING

*American table manners are, if anything, a more advanced
form of civilized behavior than the European,
because they are more complicated and further removed from the
practical result, always a sign of refinement.*

— JUDITH MARTIN

Ask a Frenchman why the table is set with the spoons placed bowl down and forks laid tines down, and the answer will be "It has always been that way!"

Flatware as we know it today effectively came into use at the end of the 17th century in France. The oldest patterns such as Trifid were engraved with crests and monograms on the backs of stems and handles so that they might be seen when set on the table, which indicates that indeed, it has been done that way for centuries.

Since forks and knives for eating were new to diners at the royal court, it was natural that they would treat them in much the same way that they handled carving utensils. The fork went in the left hand to hold down food while the knife in the right hand cut it. It certainly was a sensible and an efficient way to convey food from plate to mouth.

However, in the mid-18th century, when table cutlery became commonly accepted by the British, new rules and rituals developed and affectations prevailed. Little fingers went up in the air when forks were switched to the right hand after cutting, and knives were put down when not in use. Emily Post later referred to this as "zigzag eating," which was considered the fashionable and proper way to use forks and knives. But in France, tradition has prevailed; forks, knives, and spoons are their original size (about an inch longer than the Anglo); monograms and decorative designs are still placed on the back. Of course, we can mimic the style without the monogrammed silver.

CHICKEN CHILI

Comforting food like chili is usually served up in a bowl or a big mug. The addition of an elegant silver cream soup spoon makes it a little more special.

¼ cup olive oil

2 Spanish onions, in large chunks

4 to 6 garlic cloves, sliced

1 each yellow and red bell peppers, diced 1 jalapeño pepper, minced

1 tablespoon red pepper flakes

2 tablespoons ground chili powder

1 teaspoon black pepper

Salt to taste

2 cans (28 ounces each) whole plum tomatoes, drained and coarsley chopped

2 tablespoons red wine vinegar

1 can (1 pound) red kidney beans, with liquid

1 can (1 pound) pinto or white kidney beans, with liquid

¼ cup cornmeal

5 whole chicken breasts, skinned and boned, poached in chicken or vegetable stock

1 bunch parsley, chopped

Sour cream, chopped scallions, and grated sharp Cheddar cheese, for garnish

In a heavy 8-quart stockpot, heat the olive oil. When hot, sauté the onions, garlic, peppers, and jalapeño for 5 minutes, until they start to brown. Then add the pepper flakes, chili powder, black pepper, and salt. Cook for a few minutes longer.

Add the tomatoes and vinegar; cook for about 10 minutes.

Add the beans and simmer for about 15 minutes.

In a small bowl, combine the cornmeal with a ladleful of liquid from the pot; add the mixture back into the chili.

Tear the chicken into strips, add to the chili along with the parsley and simmer until hot.

Serve in a bowl, cup, or mug with garnishes on the side.

SERVES 8 TO 10

The sterling silver cream soup spoon is from James Robinson.

SALADS

FRESH GREEN SALAD was a luxury first introduced to the dinner table by the French in the 1800s. It was a simple lettuce salad, the leaves torn and dressed with oil and vinegar before being brought to the table. Etiquette dictated that salad must never be cut with a knife; the steel blades would give off a metallic taste and discolor the lettuce. So the French eat their greens using only a silver fork.

The elegant antique French salad servers, with horn or bone on the working end and handles of silver or silver plate, were developed for the express purpose of serving without having metal touch the dressed salad. You can find these beautiful and usable servers today, sometimes in an original leather box, if you search the shops and

antique markets of Paris. They're very difficult to find elsewhere.

It wasn't until the latter part of the 19th
century, when technology made it possible
to transport fresh produce from farm to
market, that fresh salad found its way to the
English table. But it was still a luxury, and
the affluent Victorian host and hostess
enjoyed nothing more than serving luxury
foods with specific utensils.

English salad forks had one tine wider
than the rest, for cutting tender leaves. There
were long-handled forks with three sharp
tines for serving lettuce. Tomato spoons were
pierced; tomato servers had slots. And of

course there were specific implements for
countless condiments: relish forks, pickle
forks, and olive forks, often with carved
bone, ivory, or mother-of-pearl handles.

When collecting and shopping today, the
lines can be blurred between a salad fork, a
pastry fork, or a fish fork—for good reason.
They all have a wide left tine, they're all
smaller than a dinner fork, and silver manufacturers often used the same design, calling
it by different names in different patterns.
So when you find a set of forks that you
love at an antique show and they look like
salad forks, buy them and use them for
salad, or pastry, or fish.

PAGE 66: *Traditional French salad servers have polished horn or bone on the working end and silver on the handles.*
OPPOSITE: *An olive spoon has a pierced bowl to allow oil or brine to drain off.*

TOP: *An English silver fork in the Military Fiddle Thread pattern is engraved with a deer crest.*
On the plate are Ina Garten's couscous and roasted carrots. ABOVE: *An array of useful forks: an olive fork, a hot meat fork, a*
baked-potato fork, a fork of steel and bone, an ornate silver serving fork, two pickle forks (one bone, the other bone and silver),
a lettuce fork, a sardine fork, and a fish serving fork.

BAREFOOT CONTESSA'S CURRIED COUSCOUS

We always found couscous intimidating until Ina Garten shared her recipe with us. Serve this up with your largest and most ornate silver vegetable spoon as a side dish with meat or poultry, or with other salads for lunch.

3 cups water
1 pound (2¼ cups) couscous
½ cup raisins
4 tablespoons butter

DRESSING
1½ teaspoons turmeric
1⅓ tablespoons curry powder
½ cup olive oil
¾ cup white wine vinegar
1 teaspoon salt
1 teaspoon pepper
1 pint plain yogurt
⅓ cup each *finely minced carrots, red onion, cucumber, and scallions*
¼ cup slivered almonds, toasted

Bring the water to a boil. In a bowl, combine the couscous and raisins. Melt the butter in the boiling water, then pour over the couscous. Let sit for 20 to 30 minutes, until the water is absorbed. Fluff with a fork.

Make the dressing by whisking all the dressing ingredients together. Pour enough dressing over the couscous to moisten it lightly, then toss.

Add the minced vegetables and almonds and toss again.

SERVES 8 TO 10

BAREFOOT CONTESSA'S ROASTED CARROTS

Serve with your prize slotted tomato server or a pierced berry spoon.

10 carrots, peeled
¼ cup olive oil
Salt and pepper to taste
¼ cup chopped fresh dill

Preheat oven to 400°F. Slice the carrots on the diagonal, about ⅓ inch thick. Toss with the oil and salt and pepper. Spread on a baking sheet and bake for 20 minutes, until tender and nicely browned.

Toss with dill and serve warm or at room temperature.

SERVES 4 TO 6

VINAIGRETTE

A light dressing, good for summer salads, steamed vegetables such as asparagus, and fish dishes.

3 garlic cloves, minced
Salt and pepper
1 tablespoon Dijon mustard
2 teaspoons sugar
⅓ cup fresh lemon juice
⅔ cup olive oil

In a ceramic or glass bowl, mash the garlic with the salt. Add the pepper, mustard, sugar, and lemon juice. Mix with a fork or small whisk. Slowly drizzle the oil into the mixture, whisking all the while.

MAKES 1¼ CUPS

Variation 1: This is good with light spicy and Oriental foods. Substitute ⅓ cup rice wine vinegar for the lemon juice.

Variation 2: This heavier, full-flavored dressing is good with meat and game. Substitute ⅓ cup balsamic vinegar for the lemon juice.

ABOVE: *Pierced silver asparagus server in the English Fiddle Thread and Shell pattern.* OPPOSITE: *The small Tiffany sterling sauce ladle being used to serve vinaigrette is in the style of the Old English pattern.*

SILVER HOLDERS AND SERVERS

In the first place, queerly shaped pieces of flat silver,
contrived for purposes known only to their designers, have no place
on a well-appointed table. So if you use one of these implements for
a purpose not intended, it cannot be a breach of etiquette.
— EMILY POST

The French were using silver holders and servers for food even before the British were setting their tables with forks and knives.

There were fat silver handles with turnscrews to hold a lamb bone steady while carving a leg. There were gadgets for ham bones and tiny silver holders for pigeon legs, and little clamps to steady escargots.

Yet when the British started devising new gadgets for the new foods that graced their tables in the 1860s, they had no equal. Asparagus in particular were honored, with servers of silver with piercing, chasing, monogramming,

and engraving. There were even little individual "plyers" for holding and eating one asparagus at a time. Sandwich and steak servers may have been exactly the same as their asparagus cousins, but called by a different name.

There were scissors-like silver snips for cutting a chunk off a cone of sugar. But tongs for serving lumps of sugar came in an enormous array of patterns and styles. A favorite shape for the working end seemed to be a griffin's paw. Larger than what we think sugar tongs should be, they make handsome ice tongs for our 20th-century tables.

TOP: *A collection of griffin paw sugar tines pressed into service as ice tongs.* ABOVE: *At a formal French dinner, Aude Clément uses individual silver escargot and pigeon holders.*

An ornate Christofle silver-plate fork pairs well with a simple hollow-handle knife. The salad is a mix of thinly sliced fennel and shaved Parmesan.

PEAR VINAIGRETTE

2 or 3 medium pears
¾ teaspoon fresh dill
1½ teaspoons coarse-grain mustard
2 teaspoons cider vinegar
1 tablespoon fresh lemon juice
2 tablespoons sugar
½ cup salad oil
Salt and pepper

Peel and core the pears. Puree them in a food processor until smooth. Strain out any lumps and measure out 1 cup. Return to the processor along with the dill, mustard, vinegar, lemon juice, and sugar. Blend until smooth. Very slowly, drizzle in the oil, until just blended. Be very cautious when mixing the ingredients, as the dressing should only emulsify, not thicken. Add salt and pepper to taste before serving.

MAKES 1½ CUPS

OPPOSITE TOP: *Another Victorian folly—olive and pickle forks with ivory and bone handles.* FAR LEFT: *A reproduction of the classic French salad servers.* LEFT: *A bone-handled butter knife with chasing on the silver blade is above the plate of romaine and beet salad.*

ROMAINE, BEETS, AND ROQUEFORT

A pretty salad is most appetizing when eaten with a gleaming silver salad fork and knife, bone-handled fish eaters, or a dessert set.

6 medium beets, peeled and cut into ½-inch julienne
1 cup balsamic vinegar
3 tablespoons dark brown sugar
1 teaspoon salt
Romaine, trimmed, washed, and dried
Roquefort cheese, broken into bite-sized pieces
Vinaigrette Variation 1 (page 72)

To pickle the beets, put the beets, vinegar, brown sugar, and salt in a saucepan and add water to cover. Bring to a boil, reduce the heat, and simmer until fork-tender, about 10 minutes. Set aside to cool.

Place the beets in a jar, cover with the pickling liquid, and refrigerate until needed.

To make the salad, arrange 4 or 5 romaine leaves in a fan shape on a salad plate. Place 6 to 8 beet strips at the base of the fan. Sprinkle with Roquefort and drizzle with vinaigrette.

FIELD MUSHROOM SALAD

These large, meaty mushrooms are a very substantial part of a cold meal. Serve them with a broad three- or four-tined serving fork and a small coin silver spoon for the juice.

Juice of 2 lemons

5 tablespoons extra-virgin olive oil

1 garlic clove, smashed, peeled, and chopped

2 teaspoons powdered bay leaf

4 whole bay leaves

8 whole cardamom pods

6 large field mushrooms, peeled

Salt and pepper

In a sauté pan, bring to a boil the lemon juice, olive oil, garlic, powdered bay leaf, whole bay leaves, and cardamom pods. Turn down the heat and simmer for 3 minutes. Add the mushrooms and simmer them for 5 minutes on each side, covered.

Pour into a ceramic bowl and cool. Cover with plastic wrap and refrigerate a few hours or overnight. Strain before serving and add salt and pepper to taste.

SERVES 6

OPPOSITE: *Horn and ivory antique French salad servers with ornate silver handles.* ABOVE: *It was typical of silver sets in the Old English pattern for knives to have ivory or bone handles.*

MAIN COURSES

TRADITIONALLY THE MAIN course was a meat served with accompaniments of potatoes and a vegetable or two, eaten with the dinner fork and knife. There was no confusion: The dinner fork was the largest of the place-setting forks. The dinner knife was not only the largest but the sharpest knife for cutting meat.

Today, our main course is as likely to be fish or fowl, pasta or vegetables, as it is to be meat. Yet it is still comforting and reassuring to eat our main course—the middle and heartiest course—with the largest fork and knife.

The fun in collecting here may be in the variety of patterns and types of handles you can find. You might spot early sterling in a classic pattern like Fiddle and Thread. The ornate King's pattern was originally of sterling, later copied in silver plate. There are bone-handled and horn-handled forks with silver tines, and their companion knives with steel blades and silver cuffs. There are forks and knives with handles of wood, as rare as ebony or common as cocoa wood, with steel designs riveted through the wood to secure them to the steel blades and tines.

At American antique markets, you can find sets of forks and knives with plastic handles of such an early vintage that they still have carbon steel blades. There you can also find Art Deco kitchen cutlery with colorful Bakelite handles and stainless steel on the working end. In England, you can find handsome faux ivory or bone knives with steel blades and their companion forks of silver plate.

The dinner fork and dinner knife are the grandparents of all cutlery. When you find a set of cutlery in its original box, no matter what vintage, it will always include dinner forks and knives. Other place pieces are a reflection of the fashions of the time, the whim of the manufacturer, and the wealth of the purchaser.

PAGE 82: *An array of antique dinner cutlery fills a cast-iron urn. At the base, an English carving set of natural horn with silver cuffs and tips, steel tines and blade.* OPPOSITE: *An ornate silver serving spoon and fork, circa 1860.*

STEEL TINES
AND BLADES

When the ducks and the green peas
came we looked at each other
with dismay; we had only two-pronged,
black-handled forks. It's true, the
steel was bright as silver; but what
were we to do?

— ELIZABETH CLEGHORN GASKELL

For those who couldn't afford silver, carbon steel was the metal most often used for tines and blades. Handles were made of non–heat-conducting wood or horn. Rivets of steel, in decorative shapes, fastened the handles to the shaft of the blades and tines.

Because it holds a sharp edge, steel was used to make the blades of knives used for cutting meat, even when the handles were of silver. But carbon steel corrodes when in contact with acid foods, such as lemon and vinegar; therefore fork tines and the blades of knives for eating fruit and fish were made of silver.

The steel blades on these knives are proudly stamped
with the makers name and CUTLER TO HIS MAJESTY.

HOWARD'S TUNA STEAK

Here is the perfect dish to enjoy with your most beautiful fish eaters. This flavorful recipe is one of our favorites at the house of our friends Howard and Gail Adler.

20 pearl onions
6 small Yukon Gold potatoes
4 tablespoons olive oil
Tuna steaks (8 ounces each),
1½ inches thick
Salt and pepper
1 teaspoon sugar
½ cup red wine
¼ cup red wine vinegar
2 tablespoons fish or vegetable stock
2 tablespoons butter
4 scallions, sliced lengthwise

Boil the onions in water to cover for 3 minutes. Drain, cut off the root end, and pinch off the skin.

Boil the potatoes in water to cover until fork-tender, drain, and cut in thick slices. Keep warm.

In a heavy skillet, heat 2 tablespoons of the olive oil until hot. Sprinkle the tuna with salt and pepper to taste, then sear the steaks in the oil for 2 minutes on each side over high heat (for rare tuna). Remove to a warm serving platter or dinner plates.

Add the remaining 2 tablespoons of olive oil to the same pan. When it is hot, add the boiled onions and glaze by shaking the pan for 3 minutes. Stir in the sugar, wine, and vinegar; bring to a boil; and cook until reduced to a thick syrup. Stir in the stock and add the butter to bind the sauce.

Put the potato slices on a platter with the tuna and spoon the sauce over. Garnish with the scallions.

SERVES 2

ABOVE: *The sauce spoon was introduced in the late 20th century by a French restaurateur for scooping up every last bit of delicious sauce; it pairs well with a typical English fish set.*

GRILLED PORK TENDERLOIN

Lots of flavor here, with few calories and loads of satisfaction. Bread forks work wonderfully on the small rounds of pork tenderloin, which can be served hot or at room temperature.

*4 pork tenderloins, trimmed
of any fat*
4 teaspoons brown sugar
2 teaspoons Coleman's dry mustard
1 ounce rum
4 teaspoons Dijon mustard
5 garlic cloves, finely minced
4 shakes Tabasco
1 tablespoon olive oil
Salt and pepper

Put the pork in a shallow ceramic bowl and set aside.

Dissolve the brown sugar and dry mustard in the rum. Combine with the remaining ingredients and pour over the pork. Cover the dish with plastic wrap and let the pork marinate in the refrigerator for 30 minutes or more.

Preheat a grill to hot and cook the tenderloins, turning frequently, for about 20 minutes or until done. You can also bake these at 375°F. To serve, slice on the bias ½ inch thick.

SERVES 8

An antique silver three-tined silver bread fork, made to mimic twigs, serves up the grilled pork.

THE BEAUTY OF BAKELITE

When Bakelite was first introduced in the early 20th century, it mimicked expensive natural materials like ivory, bone, and tortoiseshell. In the Deco era it developed a life of its own. Young industrial designers created original designs in odd shapes and bright colors for kitchen cutlery. Paired with newly invented stainless steel, this was truly modern stuff!

With heat-resistant handles and corrosion-resistant blades, bowls, and tines, Bakelite seemed impervious to all the elements. Then dishwashers came along. The high water and drying temperatures changed the colors and dulled its glow, and that was the end of Bakelite as a practical material.

Since it wasn't considered valuable, most kitchen cutlery was damaged or discarded. Bakelite's now being noticed—not quite antique, but charming.

Bakelite is easy to mix and match, as is evident in Peter Hoffman and Susan Rosenfeld's collection used at Savoy, their restaurant in New York City.

PASTA WITH BROCCOLI RABE AND TURKEY SAUSAGE

Use your large silver dinner fork and a European dessert spoon for eating this hearty and healthy pasta.

*2 bunches broccoli rabe,
thick ends removed*

Salt

*8 links turkey sausage,
cut into 1-inch slices*

¼ cup olive oil

5 garlic cloves, thinly sliced

Black pepper

1 teaspoon crushed red pepper

1 pound thin linguine

Freshly grated Parmesan cheese

Cut the broccoli rabe into bite-sized pieces. Boil in salted water for 8 minutes. Drain and set aside.

Sauté the sausage slices in a little oil until brown and cooked through. Set aside.

In a heavy skillet, sauté the garlic in some oil with salt, pepper, and crushed red pepper until the garlic is tan. Add the rabe and cook for 8 minutes.

Meanwhile, cook the linguine in well-salted boiling water until al dente. Add ½ cup pasta water to the rabe. Drain the pasta and put in individual bowls. Top with the broccoli rabe sauce and sausage. Serve with Parmesan.

SERVES 4 TO 6

OPPOSITE: *Silver-plate cream soup spoons are paired with late 19th-century resin-handled steel forks and knives for dishing up pasta with rabe and sausage.* ABOVE: *A Victorian treasure—a fork just for serving baked potatoes.*

GRILLED VEGETABLES

We serve this as an antipasto with bread and cheeses for our vegetarian friends. For a crowd we add platters of cold meats and fish, using our largest four-tined silver serving fork and Victorian vegetable spoon.

3 fennel bulbs, trimmed and cut in ½-inch slices

6 new potatoes, in ½-inch slices

6 bell peppers, yellow and red, in strips, seeds removed

1 medium eggplant, in ½-inch rounds

3 small yellow squash, in ½-inch slices, lengthwise

3 small zucchini, halved lengthwise

3 medium onions, peeled and cut in ½-inch slices

Olive oil
Salt and pepper
Fresh thyme or rosemary sprigs

Parboil the fennel and potatoes in boiling salted water for 8 minutes.

Fire up the grill. Brush all the vegetables with olive oil and sprinkle with salt and pepper. Grill one kind of vegetable at a time so you can judge doneness, and cook only until fork-tender.

Arrange on a large serving platter and garnish with sprigs of fresh thyme or rosemary. Serve at room temperature.

SERVES 6

ABOVE: *Grilled vegetables are served with vintage Victorian flea market tablespoons and a dinner fork.*

ROASTED GARLIC

*Roasted garlic is mild and creamy.
Use your antique silver
butter knives or resin-handled tea knives
to spread it on bread.*

*1 head garlic
Salt and pepper
Olive oil*

Preheat the oven to 350° F.

Cut the top third off the head of garlic, to expose all the cloves. Place on a baking tray, sprinkle with salt and pepper, and drizzle with olive oil. Bake for ½ hour. Drizzle with a little more olive oil and continue to bake until brown and bubbly, about ½ hour more.

Serve hot or at room temperature.

SERVE 1 WHOLE HEAD PER PERSON

TWO-MEAT MEAT LOAF

*A cross between a meat loaf and a pâté,
this is one of our favorite warm-weather dishes.*

*2 pounds lean ground beef
1 pound cooked ham, ground
2 eggs, beaten
1½ cups
seasoned bread crumbs
1 teaspoon fresh thyme leaves plus
sprigs for garnish
2 tablespoons cognac
2 teaspoons salt
1 teaspoon freshly ground
black pepper
Honey mustard for serving*

Preheat the oven to 350° F.

In a bowl, mix all the ingredients well using your hands. Press into the bowl to form an even mound, then turn out on a foil-covered baking sheet. Bake for 1½ hours.

Serve thinly sliced with honey mustard, at room temperature. Garnish with sprigs of fresh thyme.

SERVES 8

A Victorian bread fork is recycled as a meat fork.

BREAD FORKS

*Wait and see; one day
you each will have a fork. Mark
my words!*

— THOMAS CORYANTE

A short-lived affectation of the Victorian English table was the three-tine bread fork. Its sole purpose was removing bread and rolls from service plate to individual bread and butter plate without touching it with one's fingers.

No two handles were alike. Some were fat, some skinny, some elaborate, some plain as bread. Their only common ground was the three pointed silver tines.

There remains a wide variety of these peculiar forks in antique shops and markets today, ours for the buying. Most have seen little use and are in very good condition. Sturdy enough for serving hot and cold meats, the intriguing shape is a welcome addition to any table.

Typical three-tined bread forks, one with an ivory handle and silver cuffs and tines; the other boasts a natural-horn handle with a silver cuff and unusually shaped tines.

MIXED FISH GRILL

This is a great company fish dinner.
Those who don't like all fish can pick and choose,
aided by a set of Victorian fish servers.

3 tablespoons mixed chopped herbs
(basil, thyme, rosemary, sage, parsley)
½ cup olive oil
Salt and pepper
1 pound salmon fillets
1 pound tuna fillets
1 pound swordfish fillets

In a large shallow bowl, mix the herbs with the oil and salt and pepper to taste. Add the fish fillets and marinate for ½ hour at room temperature.

Preheat an outdoor grill and brush it lightly with oil. Grill the fish for 6 to 8 minutes per side, depending on the thickness. Baste often with the marinade.

SERVES 6

ABOVE: *An unusual solid-handle, silver-plate fish knife in the Old English Bead pattern, used with a fish fork of ivory and silver.*

WILD MUSHROOMS AND PASTA

An easy, earthy, and elegant pasta requires elegant cutlery. An ornate Victorian or simple Fiddle pattern fork and an accompanying oval tablespoon will enhance your eating pleasure.

Salt

4 garlic cloves, thinly sliced

¼ cup olive oil

1 pound any mix of fresh exotic mushrooms (morel, oyster, porcini, shiitake, chanterelles), sliced

Pepper

½ cup medium-sweet Madeira

1 pound thin linguine

¼ cup chopped fresh parsley

Bring a large pot of salted water to a boil.

In a large heavy skillet, sauté the garlic in the oil until lightly golden. Add the mushrooms, salt, and pepper and sauté for 5 minutes. Add the Madeira, cook for 7 minutes, then stir in ½ cup water from the pasta pot.

Cook and drain the pasta. Put in individual bowls and top with the mushrooms and sauce. Garnish with chopped parsley.

SERVES 4 TO 6

ABOVE: *A resin-handle steel fork is a pleasing contrast to the ornate mid-19th-century dessert spoon.*

BURN-THE-HOUSE-DOWN
CHICKEN

The garlic lover's way to warm the house on a cold evening and prepare a great dinner at the same time. Don't leave this chicken alone—the name is a warning! Vintage cutlery with steel tines and blades and wood or bone handles has that old homey look that goes well with roasted chicken.

1 lemon, cut in half

1 roasting chicken (3 pounds)

5 garlic cloves

Coarse salt and pepper

Preheat the oven to 500° F.

Squeeze half the lemon inside and half on the outside of the chicken. Smash, peel, and coarsely chop the garlic. Rub the bird inside and out with the garlic. Sprinkle generously with salt and pepper inside and out. Place the chicken, breast side up, on a rack in a roasting pan and roast for 1 hour without opening the oven door.

Cut in half and place on a platter or individual plates.

SERVES 2 GENEROUSLY

ABOVE AND OPPOSITE: *Steel forks and knives with handles of coca wood came in a wide variety of rivet designs in the late 19th century, when they were offered through the Sears, Roebuck and Montgomery Ward catalogs for about $1.50 per set of six.*

DESSERTS

AS EARLY AS the 11th century, forks were used for eating ginger, berries, and fruits that might stain the fingers. Dessert cutlery was not just a Victorian whim, but an embellishment on history. And what an embellishment!

When browsing through antique shops, you may come across sets of berry forks, with two long skinny tines, very much like their 11th-century ancestors. Typical of the Victorian era are dessert forks and knives with ivory, bone, or mother-of-pearl handles, their silver blades and tines often embellished with chasing. You will find that they are very similar to fish sets, only smaller and with fewer curves to the knife blade.

There are sets of late-Victorian dessert knives with beautifully colored resin handles of purple, turquoise, chartreuse, and ochre with silver blades and cuffs. On our tables today, we can use them for butter at breakfast, cheese at cocktail time, or fruit for dessert. There are pie servers, cake servers, and cake slicers. There are ice-cream forks and ice-cream spoons—said to be an American invention. There are citrus fruit spoons with pointed bowls, and sauce spoons with one flat scalloped edge, which makes scooping up the last drop of sauce seem polite. There are pastry forks with one wider tine for cutting crust. And our favorite collectible, the large English dessert spoon, which we employ for eating soup, pasta, and of course dessert.

To the very end of the meal spoons prevail, with tiny demitasse spoons and coffee spoons, tea spoons, four o'clock tea spoons, and iced tea spoons. And saving the best for last, there are bonbon spoons, for passing on that last little sweet.

PAGE 102: *Antique and new dessert forks, knives, and spoons poke out of a pound cake atop a pressed-glass cake stand.* OPPOSITE: *Some coin silver spoons are dainty enough to use for stirring espressos.*

CHRISTINE'S CHOCOLATE CAKE

*An extravagant silver dessert fork deserves
a cake like Christine de Beaupre's.*

4 ounces semisweet chocolate
4 ounces bitter chocolate
1 cup unsalted butter
5 eggs, separated
Salt
1¾ cups brown sugar (do not pack)
¾ cup flour

Preheat the oven to 350°F. and grease a
9×5×3-inch cake pan.

Melt the chocolate in a double boiler,
stirring frequently. Remove from the heat.
Melt the butter.

Beat the egg whites with a sprinkle of salt
until gentle peaks form. Mix together the
brown sugar, egg yolks, flour, and melted
butter and chocolate until they are well
blended. Carefully fold in the egg whites.
Pour into the cake pan and bake for about
25 minutes. The cake should stay wet in the
middle. (Test with a cake tester.)

SERVES 8

ABOVE: *A French grandmother's collection of vintage silver spoons and forks for a very French chocolate cake.*

CHRISTI CARTER'S
THREE-BERRY COBBLER

A wonderful way to enjoy the fresh fruits of summer. Our friends have been raving since last summer. This cobbler tastes best when served with a large vintage silver spoon.

½ cup butter

2 cups all-purpose flour

1 teaspoon baking powder

1½ cups granulated sugar

1¼ cups heavy cream

3 pints of any combination of
blueberries, raspberries, and
blackberries, picked over and rinsed

¼ cup brown sugar

Preheat the oven to 350° F.

Melt the butter in a 10-inch ceramic baking dish.

Mix together the flour, the baking powder, and ¾ cup of the granulated sugar. Add the cream and mix until thoroughly moist. Spoon the batter over the butter.

In a saucepan, combine the berries, brown sugar, and ¼ cup of the granulated sugar. Warm over medium heat, then pour the mixture over the dough. Sprinkle the top with the remaining ½ cup sugar. Bake until the crust rises to the top and turns golden, about 50 minutes.

Serve with softly whipped cream or ice cream.

SERVES 8

A Deco silver spoon with a shovellike bowl is used to serve the cobbler.

FRUIT FORKS,
KNIVES & SPOONS

The first piece of cutlery used to carry food
to the mouth was said to be the "suckett"
fork. These small forks, which had two long
pointed tines, were used by the ancient
Romans for eating sticky preserved ginger
and berries that might stain fingers.

Centuries later, in the royal courts of
England and France, before cutlery was
used for most foods, there were special
forks and knives for fruit only. They were
made of silver or gold so as not to impart a
metallic taste.

Today, we have a large inheritance of
fruit silver to pick and choose from. Slotted
berry spoons, deep-bowl fruit salad spoons,
individual citrus spoons, melon spoons,
knives with narrow pointed silver blades for
paring fruit, and forks for eating and serving—all are still useful on our tables today.

LEFT: *The bowl of a silver fruit spoon is embossed
with berries.* OVERLEAF: *The handles of the fruit knives
are made of resin.*

TUSCAN FRUIT AND
BREAD TART

*This may be the world's tastiest way
to use leftover bread. You can
substitute apples for the pears, or use a
combination. A pie server is ideal for cutting and
serving this tart. A cake or salad
fork with one tine wider than the rest is the best
tool for eating a portion.*

¼ *cup raisins*

2 *tablespoons rum*

3 *eggs*

2½ *cups milk*

⅓ *cup plus 1 tablespoon sugar*

Pinch of salt

Zest of 1 lemon

2 *tablespoons all-purpose flour*

2 *tablespoons cornmeal*

1 *large loaf stale country bread,
sliced ½ inch thick*

2 *pears, peeled, cored, and sliced
lengthwise*

10 *seedless red grapes, cut in half*

2 *tablespoons coarsely chopped
fresh rosemary*

1 *tablespoon olive oil*

1 *rosemary sprig for garnish*

OPPOSITE: *The bright-cut silver pie server was produced
in the 1920s.* ABOVE RIGHT: *One of life's little
niceties—sterling silver grape shears.*

Soak the raisins in the rum for 10 minutes. Beat together the eggs, ½ cup of the milk, ⅓ cup of the sugar, the salt, lemon zest, flour, and cornmeal. Soak the sliced bread in the remaining 2 cups milk for a few minutes.

Preheat the oven to 375° F.

Oil an 11-inch tart pan and lay the soaked bread in it, pressing the bread into the sides of the pan. Arrange the pear slices with the wider part around the pan's outer edges, the narrow end toward the center. Scatter the soaked raisins and the grapes around the top and sprinkle with the chopped rosemary and the remaining 1 tablespoon of sugar. Drizzle with olive oil.

Bake for 40 minutes or until golden. Lay a sprig of rosemary on top and serve warm.

SERVES 6 TO 8

CHOCOLATE CREAM POTS

*A great, very easy chocolate lovers' dessert—
and the perfect place to use those gorgeous demitasse spoons you just couldn't resist buying.*

1½ cups milk

2 eggs, lightly beaten

2 cups semisweet chocolate bits

2 teaspoons rum

3 tablespoons sugar

Salt

Heat the milk just to the boiling point. Put
all the other ingredients in the container of
a blender. Add the hot milk and blend at
low speed for 1 minute. Stir with a rubber
spatula to remove any bubbles. Pour into
10 *pot de crème* cups or any small, pretty
glasses. Chill for several hours.

SERVES 10

*Vermeil demitasse spoons are just the right size for scooping
chocolate cream from pigeon tureens.*

CHEESE KNIVES AND SCOOPS

*People who know nothing about cheese reel
away from Camembert, Roquefort, and
Stilton because the plebeian proboscis is not
equipped to differentiate between the sordid
and the sublime.*

— HARVEY DAY

It was the French who invented the special
tool just for cutting and serving firm cheese.
With a blade sharp enough to cut, the knife
end was curved down into two sharp tines
for impaling and passing a chunk. For soft-
ripe cheese there are myriad handsome
knives to spread it with. These individual
cheese knives are a hybrid: larger than a
butter knife, with the curvy pointed end of
a fish knife.

Then there's the Stilton scoop—the
work of the English—which removed
smooth round cylinders of ripe cheese without cutting into the hard rind.

OPPOSITE: *A natural-horn handle adds a masculine
touch to the chased-silver Stilton scoop.*

TEA

Teatime is filled with rituals, traditional foods, and all sorts of silver paraphernalia to help in the service of both.

It begins with the "tea" spoons that are part of every set of silverware. But what about the scallop-shaped spoon with the short stout handle? It's to scoop tea from tin to pot. There are dozens of variations on the shell-pattern bowl of this little spoon, which can make itself quite useful for serving sugar, jam, or clotted cream.

Tea knives are for spreading jam on scones. The 19th-century ones look elegant with handles of ivory or mother-of-pearl; the newer ones are bright with colored Bakelite handles. Almost all share the tradition of silver blades and cuffs.

Teatime is such a cozy hour, with comforting food that reminds many of us of the nursery. What better occasion to put to use the baby silver?

There are tea strainers of many styles; some are all silver; others have turned-wood handles; others, mother-of-pearl handles; some sit in a caddie; and others have caddies attached.

TOP: *Baby spoons and tea scoops serve jam; silver knives with chasing serve the butter and cheese.* ABOVE LEFT: *Silver dessert forks in the King's pattern with union shell.* ABOVE RIGHT: *Silver-plate fruit forks with carved bone handles and silver cuffs.* OPPOSITE: *A 1920s baby fork and spoon with an embossed puppy, a Bakelite-handled fork, and an array of traditional sterling baby spoons.*

CARE, CLEANING, STORAGE

SILVER AND SILVER PLATE

CARE. There are elements that don't agree with silver. Salt and salt air will pit silver, so if you live by the sea, keep your silver in silversmith cloth bags or in a lined silver chest when you're not using it. Some foods are also a problem. The acid in lemons and vinegar will discolor silver almost on contact; sulfur in eggs makes silver taste metallic and will also discolor it. So either avoid using silver with these foods or wash it as soon as possible after you use it.

STORING. Drawers and chests lined with Pacific Silvercloth or silversmith cloth are the best prevention against tarnish, which is caused by sulfur in the air. You can buy the cloth at a hardware or housewares store and cut, fit and glue it to line your existing drawers. Be sure to use a non-sulfur glue, or the sulfur will leach through the cloth, defeating its purpose. There are also ready-made silver drawer liners that just slip into most standard kitchen draw-

ers. They are fitted for cutlery and have a zip-closing top.

CLEANING. For very tarnished and neglected silver, most experts recommend one of the spray polishes, such as Hagerty silversmith's spray polish. These relatively new polishes are nonabrasive and are especially good for cleaning intricate patterns. They also act as a tarnish preventative.

POLISHING. According to Edward Munvees at James Robinson silversmiths in New York, rubbing and polishing are essential for maintaining the sheen and glow of silver. If your silver is used on a regular basis, it should need no more than washing in warm soapy water, rinsing, and drying with a soft dishtowel. Rubbing with a silver cloth or a soft clean cloth (such as an old undershirt) will give silver that warm cared-for shine, without making it look overpolished.

WASHING. It *is* best to wash all silver by hand and dry it at once with a soft cloth.

PAGE 120: *A showy way to store and display flea market finds in the kitchen or dining room is in turn-of-the-century pressed-glass celery urns.* RIGHT: *It's best to clean engraved and bright-cut silver with a spray polish and a treated silver cloth.*

CLOCKWISE, FROM TOP LEFT: *Handles from odd pieces of Victorian cutlery are turned into bottle openers. Silver should be rinsed in warm water and dried right away. The wood and bone handles of bread knives develop a fine patina over time. Show off the interesting handles or working ends of vintage cutlery.*

However, you can wash forks and spoons in the dishwasher. For best results, here is a tip from Mr. Munvees for loading silver in the dishwasher (though he would prefer you wash it by hand). Keep spoons and forks separate, because the water bouncing off the fork tines will spot the bowls of the spoons.

Knives are actually two separate parts, the silver handle and the steel blade, which are soldered together. For two reasons they should never be soaked or washed in the dishwasher. One, the heat of the water will, over time, compromise the union between handle and blade. Two, there is an electrolytic reaction set up between silver and steel, which causes steel to pit.

IVORY, BONE, HORN, MOTHER-OF-PEARL, WOOD

CARE AND WASHING. All cutlery with decorative handles will be damaged by soaking in water or by machine-washing. Water will cause the union between the organic handle and the metal blade to loosen. Wood, if soaked, will absorb water and crack when it dries. Ivory, bone, horn, and mother-of-pearl are very sensitive to extremes in temperature; hot water or soaking will irreparably damage these materials.

Wash in warm running water with a mild detergent. As with all cutlery, towel drying right away is always best.

STORING. Most ivory- or bone-handled cutlery comes from England, where house temperatures are cooler than in the United States. To prevent bone or ivory handles from cracking when you bring them back from England, it is important to keep them in a cool and moist place for a while, letting them adjust to our drier, warmer homes.

Don't store organic-handled cutlery near radiators, ovens, stoves, or hot lights. Store them in a cool drawer or cupboard or a lined cutlery tray. But remember, if a handle does crack, it's still beautiful and usable—it's just showing its age.

STEEL

CARE AND WASHING. Antique forks and knives of steel almost always have handles of wood, bone, or horn, which puts them in double jeopardy when it comes to washing and soaking. Do not soak them in water or wash them in the dishwasher, ever! It will rust the steel and crack the handles. So, after dinner, leave them on a plate out of water until you are ready to wash up. Then rinse the food off, sprinkle the steel knife blades and fork tines with a strong gritty cleanser (I use Bar Keeper's Friend), and rub with steel wool to remove any rust. The trick to preventing rust is to dry the cutlery at once and completely. A very light spritz with vegetable oil spray will give the steel a gleam and also help prevent rust.

STORING. The reason you buy these antique relics is not because they're easy to care for, but because they're great to look at, so keep them out on view! The only element that will damage the steel is water; extreme heat will damage the handles. Other than that, you can show them off and keep them handy. Store them in a divided basket on your kitchen table, or in glass or crockery jars with the handles up, to show them off, on your kitchen counter.

An old drawer divider in brass mesh is pretty enough to leave out on the kitchen table displaying vintage forks, knives, and spoons.

GLOSSARY

METALS

COIN SILVER. Silver of the standard of fineness used for coins. In England, it is sterling silver having a fineness of .925; in the United States, the standard of fineness is .900. The term "coin silver" is sometimes used instead of "silver," but usually refers to very thin and delicate spoons made before the Victorian era, often monogrammed with initials or a full name.

PEWTER. Early pewter was an alloy of 3 to 9 parts of tin and 1 part lead. It is now made of tin with a little copper and antimony, a bluish-white metallic element giving pewter its color. Antique pewter should be used only for decorative purposes, not for eating or serving food, since it contains lead.

SHEFFIELD. A type of silver-plated metal produced in Sheffield, England, composed of two or more different metals joined by fusing. When dealers refer to cutlery as "Sheffield" they are saying that it is early English silver plate and of a superior quality.

SILVER PLATE. Silverware made of a base metal that has been given a silver surface by the process of close plating or of electroplating, which was developed in the 1920s. On vintage pieces the silver surface is often worn thin, revealing the base metal.

Worn silver plate is still functional, just showing its age. It is possible to have it replated, if you prefer a new look over an aged one.

STAINLESS STEEL. Steel alloy with sufficient chromium to resist corrosion, oxidation, or rusting. The process was invented in the 1920s. Today the best quality stainless steel is referred to as 18/8, which is 18 percent chromium, 8 percent nickel, the balance made up of other steel alloys.

STEEL. Iron containing a little carbon, used for knife blades and fork tines before the invention of stainless steel. Steel corrodes and rusts when in contact with moisture.

STERLING SILVER. An alloy of silver and copper that in England has a fineness of .925 parts silver and .075 parts copper. In the United States the legal standard for sterling silver is .921 parts silver. English and Irish sterling have many hallmarks indicating the city in which it was made, the date, and the silversmith. American silver was marked with the silversmith's stamp and usually the word "sterling."

HANDLES

BAKELITE. The first synthetic plastic that wouldn't melt or catch on fire, developed in 1907 by chemist Leo Baekeland in Yonkers, New York. Made in bright and natural colors, it was used in the early 1900s for the handles of kitchen cutlery.

HOLLOW. Articles of silverware that are hollow as distinguished from solid flatware, such as the rounded handles of knives and serving pieces.

HORN. Fibrous, pointed growth on the heads of some animals which, being tough, light, and easily worked, has for centuries been used for the handles of knives and forks. Seen most often on carving forks and knives.

TOP: *A hollow-handle silver dessert set.* ABOVE LEFT: *Cheerful bright red Bakelite is eminently collectible.* ABOVE RIGHT: *The maker's mark is stamped on the back of a pewter spoon .* PAGE 128: *Silver knives, the blades decorated with chasing.*

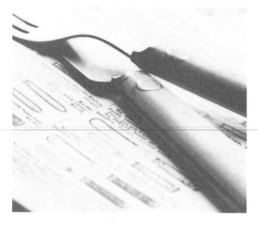

A bone-handled fork and knife.

MOTHER-OF-PEARL. Handles made of the inner layer of mollusk shells, either carved or polished. Most often found in dessert sets, fish sets, and fish servers with silver or silver-plated cuffs, blades, and tines.

RESIN. An early form of plastic used for handles. It is a clear, yellow, or brown solid substance of plant origin, often tinted bright colors for tea knives.

IVORY AND BONE. Handles of cutlery having the principal part made of ivory or bone. Both are a creamy color which darkens with age. Often carved in simple or ornate designs, they usually have tines and blades of silver or silver plate.

WOOD. Wooden handles are easier to hold than those made of heat-conducting metals. In the late 19th century, it was more economical to make steel cutlery with wood handles than other non–heat-conducting materials. The handles were often riveted to the shaft with steel decorative designs.

DECORATION

CHASING. The technique of decorating the surface of silver or silver plate by indenting it and raising the design, using a great number of differently shaped tracing tools and a chasing hammer. Chasing is coarser than engraving and can be distinguished by the blurred impression it leaves on the underside of the metal.

CUFFS. A cylindrical band covering the joint between the handle and blade of a knife or tines of a fork when they are made

of different materials. Cuffs are usually silver even if the blade and tines are of silver
plate.

ENGRAVING. The technique of decorating the surface of silver or other metals
by incising lines, monograms, patterns, or
portraits. Engraving is a special skill, done
not by a silversmith but by an engraver.

ABOVE: *Silver cuffs with resin handles.* BELOW: *The silver blades of elaborately pierced fish servers cast a lacy shadow.*

PIERCING. A type of openwork made by
piercing the metal to make a pattern of
small holes. The holes are usually circular,
but other shapes are possible. The holes are
often arranged in a decorative pattern of
various styles.

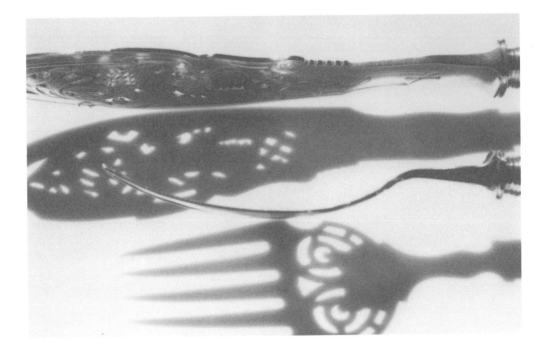

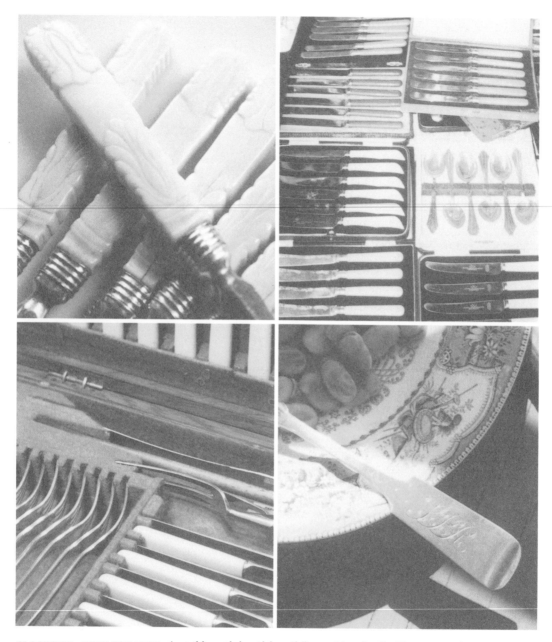

CLOCKWISE, FROM TOP LEFT: *A set of dessert forks with beautifully carved ivory handles. Various sets in their original leather boxes on display at Portobello Road Market. A coin silver serving spoon with an elegant monogram. A typical English boxed set of cutlery containing silver-plate forks and steel knives with bone handles.*

SETS

CHRISTENING SETS. Various articles intended as gifts to an infant on the ocasion of christening. A complete set would be in a lined leather presentation box that might include a knife, fork, spoon, and food pusher.

DESSERT SETS. Used at a dinner table for the dessert course served as the last course after the cheese. Such sets are usually found in sets of six in lined leather presentation boxes, and include dessert forks and dessert knives. Dessert spoons and serving spoons are most often found as sets on their own.

FISH EATERS. A conforming fish fork and fish knife to be used as a pair, each made with silver blades and tines, usually with handles of bone or ivory but sometimes of mother-of-pearl or hollow silver. Often found in the original presentation box in sets of six.

FISH SERVERS. A conforming fish fork and fish knife to be used as a pair for deboning and serving fish. The silver or silver-plated knife blade is often in the shape of a fish, decorated with chasing and piercing. Always made as a set of two, often found in its original presentation box.

FRUIT KNIVES. A type of small knife used for paring fruit, the blade being slightly curved and sharply pointed. Often made with mother-of-pearl, bone, ivory, or other ornamental handles. The blades are usually made of silver or silver plate, not steel, with silver cuffs.

TEA KNIVES. A small knife used for spreading jam or butter, the blade of silver or silver plate being rounded like a butter knife. Often made with handles of mother-of-pearl, bone, ivory, or colorful resin, with silver cuffs. Usually found in sets of six in velvet-lined leather boxes.

RESODRCES

A   *Antique*
B   *Bakelite*
MO   *Mail order*
NR   *New and reproduction cutlery*
PM   *Pattern matching service*
SP   *Silver plate*
SS   *Sterling silver*
U   *Cast-iron urns*

SHOPS

Aaron's Antiques   A SS
576 Fifth Avenue
New York, NY 10036
800-447-5868

Amy Perlin Antiques A SP
New York, NY
212-744-4923
By appointment

Balasses House Antiques A SP
Main Street and Hedges Lane
Amagansett, NY 11930
516-267-3032

Beverly Bremer Silver Shop MO PM SS
3164 Peachtree Road NE
Atlanta, GA 30305
404-261-4009

Christofle Pavilion NR SP SS
680 Madison Avenue
New York, NY 10021
(Also: Beverly Hills, Chicago, San Francisco)
212-308-9390

The Country Dining Room Antiques
A SP SS
178 Main Street
Great Barrington, MA 01230
413-528-5050

Cupboards and Roses U
Route 7, P.O. Box 426
Sheffield, MA 01257
413-229-3070

Fritz's American Wonder A B SP
At the Tomato Factory
2 Somerset Street
Hopewell, NJ 08525
609-466-9833

James Robinson A NR SS
480 Park Avenue
New York, NY 10022
212-752-6166

Jean's Silversmiths Inc. A NR SS
16 West 45th Street
New York, NY 10036
212-575-0723

Lost City Arts U
275 Lafayette Street
New York, NY 10012
212-941-8025

Lucullus A SP SS
610 Chartres Street
New Orleans, LA 70130
504-528-9620

Mood Indigo B
181 Prince Street
New York, NY 10012
212-254-1176

Piccolo Pete's Art Deco Store A B SS
13814 Ventura Boulevard
Sherman Oaks, CA 91423
818-907-9060

Rooms & Gardens Inc. U
290 Lafayette Street
New York, NY 10012
212-431-1297

Treillage Ltd. U
418 East 75th Street
New York, NY 10021
212-535-2288

Urban Archaeology Co. U
285 Lafayette Street
New York, NY 10012
212-431-6969

Wolfman • Gold & Good Company
A MO NR SP
116 Greene Street
New York, NY 10012
212-431-1888

ZigZag B
3419 North Lincoln Avenue
Chicago, IL 60657
312-525-1060

ANTIQUE MARKETS
The Pier Shows, New York City
A B SP SS U
Pier 90–92 at the Hudson River

Contact the show managers below
for exact dates of Pier shows:

McHugh Presentations
January, April, and September
617-255-9120

Sanford L. Smith & Associates
Museum of American Folk Art,
August; fall show, October
212-777-5218

Irene Stella Show Management Co.
February and November
201-384-0010

LONDON
The Dining Room Shop A SP SS
62-64 White Hart Lane
Barnes, London SW 13 OPZ
011-44-081-878-7404

Thomas Goode & Co. Ltd A NR SP SS
19 South Audley Street
London W1Y 6BN
011-44-071-499-2823

ANTIQUE MARKETS
Bermondsey Market (New Caledonian)
A SP SS U
Friday mornings, 5 A.M. to 1 P.M.
Year round, outdoors

Camden Passage A SP SS U
Islington

Wednesday, 7:30 A.M. to 2 P.M.
Saturday, 10 A.M. to 2 P.M.
Year round, indoors and outdoors

Portobello Road Market A SP SS U
Portobello Road
Saturday, 9 A.M. to 5 P.M.
Year round, indoors and outdoors

PARIS
Argenterie des Francs Bourgeois A SP SS
17, rue des Francs Bourgeois
Paris 75004
011-33-1-42 72 04 00

Au Bain Marie A NR SP SS
10, rue Boissy D'Angelas
Paris 75008
011-33-1-42 56 59 74

Au Puceron Chineur A SP SS
23, rue Saint-Paul
Paris 75004
011-33-1-42 72 88 20

Diners en Ville A NR SP SS
27, rue de Varenne
Paris 75007
011-33-1-42 22 78 33

ANTIQUE MARKETS
Marché aux Puces A SP SS U
Port de Clingancourt
Saturday, Sunday, and Monday
Year round, indoors and outdoors

SUGGESTED READING

THE VICTORIAN CATALOGUE OF HOUSEHOLD GOODS,

by Dorothy Bosomworth.
New York: Portland House, 1991.
A catalogue of more than 5,000 vintage illustrations of items used to furnish and decorate the Victorian home. Includes illustrations of cutlery that one might come across at antique markets in England, making identification great fun.

BRADBURY'S BOOK OF HALLMARKS,

by Frederick Bradbury.
Sheffield, England: J.W. Northend Ltd, 1978.
A definitive reference in paperback for marks of origin on British and Irish silver, gold, and platinum from 1544 to 1978.

FROM HAND TO MOUTH: OR HOW WE INVENTED KNIVES, FORKS, SPOONS, AND CHOPSTICKS & THE TABLE MANNERS TO GO WITH THEM,

by James Cross Giblin.
New York: Thomas Y. Crowell, 1987.
A wonderfully readable, illustrated book written for young people. It brings the development of cutlery to life.

A DIRECTORY OF AMERICAN SILVER, PEWTER, AND SILVER PLATE,

by Ralph and Terry H. Kovel.
New York: Crown Publishers, 1979.
A comprehensive listing of all known makers of silver prior to 1900. This guide makes it simple to identify the marks of every American silversmith before this century.

SILVER, A PRACTICAL GUIDE
TO COLLECTING SILVERWARE AND
IDENTIFYING HALLMARKS,
by Joel Langford.
Secaucus, N.J.: Chartwell Books, 1991.
It is exactly what the title promises. Lots of
information on marks; includes all silver
objects, not just cutlery.

AN ILLUSTRATED DICTIONARY
OF SILVERWARE,
by Harold Newman.
New York: Thames and Hudson, 1987.
Full of information on British and North
American silverware, decorative technique,
style, and design. A lot of information on
silver, not a lot on cutlery.

THE EVOLUTION OF
USEFUL THINGS,
by Henry Petroski.
New York: Alfred A. Knopf, 1992.
There are several chapters in this book
pertaining to cutlery. One, "How the Fork
Got Its Tines," gives the history of forks.
Another, "Patterns of Proliferation," tells
the story of Victorian silverware.

SILVER FLATWARE,
by Ian Pickford.
Woodbridge, Suffolk, England: Baron
Publishing, 1983.
One of the few illustrated guides for
collectors of antique flatware. Deals with the
history, evolution, style, and manufacturing
techniques from the mid-1600s to 1980.

ENCYCLOPEDIA OF AMERICAN
SILVER MANUFACTURERS,
by Dorothy T. Rainwater.
New York: Crown Publishers, 1975.
A history and reference of more than 1,400
manufacturers' names and marks, for identification of silver and silver plate from the
beginning of the Industrial Revolution on.

THE RITUALS OF DINNER,
by Margaret Visser.
New York: Grove Weidenfeld, 1991.
A fascinating book on all aspects of dining,
from food to etiquette, from plates to
chopsticks, to the evolution of forks, knives,
and spoons.

INDEX

CONVERSION CHART

EQUIVALENT IMPERIAL & METRIC MEASUREMENTS

American cooks use standard containers, the 8-ounce cup and a tablespoon that takes exactly 16 level fillings to fill that cup level. Measuring by cup makes it very difficult to give weight equivalents, as a cup of densely packed butter will weigh considerably more than a cup of flour. The easiest way therefore to deal with cup measurements in recipes is to take the amount by volume rather than by weight. Thus the equation reads:

1 cup = 240 ml = 8 fl. oz.   1/2 cup = 120 ml = 4 fl. oz.

It is possible to buy a set of American cup measures in major stores around the world.

In the States, butter is often measured in sticks. One stick is the equivalent of 8 tablespoons. One tablespoon of butter is therefore the equivalent to 1/2 ounce/15 grams.

LIQUID MEASURES

Fluid Ounces	U.S. Measures	Imperial Measures	Milliliters
	1 TSP	1 TSP	5
	2 TSP	1 DESSERTSPOON	10
1/2	1 TBS	1 TBS	14
1	2 TBS	2 TBS	28
2	1/4 CUP	4 TBS	56
4	1/2 CUP or 1/4 pint		110
5		1/4 PINT or 1 GILL	140
6	3/4 CUP		170
8	1 CUP or 1/2 PINT		225
9			250, 1/4 LITER
10	1 1/4 CUPS	1/2 PINT	280
12	1 1/2 CUPS or 3/4 PINT		340
15		3/4 PINT	420
16	2 CUPS or 1 PINT		450
18	2 1/4 CUPS		500, 1/2 LITER
20	2 1/2 CUPS	1 PINT	560
24	3 CUPS or 1 1/2 PINTS		675
25		1 1/4 PINTS	700
27	3 1/2 CUPS		750
30	3 3/4 CUPS	1 1/2 PINTS	840
32	4 CUPS or 2 PINTS or 1 QUART		900
35		1 3/4 PINTS	980
36	4 1/2 CUPS		1000, 1 LITER
40	5 CUPS or 2 1/2 PINTS	2 PINTS or 1 QUART	1120
48	6 CUPS or 3 PINTS		1350
50		2 1/2 PINTS	1400
60	7 1/2 CUPS	3 PINTS	1680
64	8 CUPS or 4 PINTS or 2 QUARTS		1800
72	9 CUPS		2000, 2 LITERS
80	10 CUPS or 5 PINTS	4 PINTS	2250
96	12 CUPS or 3 QUARTS		2700
100		5 PINTS	2800

SOLID MEASURES

U.S. and Imperial Measures		Metric Measures	
OUNCES	POUNDS	GRAMS	KILOS
1		28	
2		56	
3 1/2		100	
4	1/4	112	
5		140	
6		168	
8	1/2	225	
9		250	1/4
12	3/4	340	
16	1	450	
18		500	1/2
20	1 1/4	560	
24	1 1/2	675	
27		750	3/4
28	1 3/4	780	
32	2	900	
36	2 1/4	1000	1
40	2 1/2	1100	
48	3	1350	
54		1500	1 1/2
64	4	1800	
72	4 1/2	2000	2
80	5	2250	2 1/4
90		2500	2 1/2
100	6	2800	2 1/4

SUGGESTED EQUIVALENTS & SUBSTITUTES FOR INGREDIENTS

all-purpose flour—plain flour
arugula—rocket
beet—beetroot
confectioner's sugar—icing sugar
cornstarch—cornflour
eggplant—aubergine
granulated sugar—caster sugar
lima beans—broad beans
pearl onions—pickling onions

scallion—spring onion
shortening—white fat
squash—courgettes or marrow
unbleached flour—strong, white flour
vanilla bean—vanilla pod
zest—rind
zucchini—courgettes
light cream—single cream
heavy cream—double cream
half and half—12% fat milk

OVEN TEMPERATURE EQUIVALENTS

Fahrenheit	Celsius	Gas Mark	Description
225	110	1/4	Cool
250	130	1/2	
275	140	1	Very Slow
300	150	2	
325	170	3	Slow
350	180	4	Moderate
375	190	5	
400	200	6	Moderately Hot
425	220	7	Fairly Hot
450	230	8	Hot
475	240	9	Very Hot
500	250	10	Extremely Hot

Any broiling recipes can be used with the grill of the oven, but beware of high-temperature grills.

SPOONS AND FORKS,

ELECTRO SILVER PLATED ON BEST NICKEL SILVER

No. 6385   Engraved Old English Pattern.   Dessert Fork.

No. 6384   Old English Pattern.   Dessert Spoon

No. 6383   Fiddle Pattern.   Dessert Fork

No. 6388 Beaded Pattern. Table Spoon

No. 6387 Thread and Shell Pattern. Dessert Fork

No. 6386 Rat Tail Pattern. Dessert Spoon